THE PORTAGE POETRY SERIES

SERIES TITLES

Dear Lo
Brady Bove

Sadness of the Apex Predator
Dion O'Reilly

Do Not Feed the Animal
Hikari Miya

The Watching Sky
Judy Brackett Crowe

Let It Be Told in a Single Breath
Russell Thorburn

The Blue Divide
Linda Nemec Foster

Lake, River, Mountain
Mark B. Hamilton

Talking Diamonds
Linda Nemec Foster

Poetic People Power
Tara Bracco (ed.)

The Green Vault Heist
David Salner

There is a Corner of Someplace Else
Camden Michael Jones

Everything Waits
Jonathan Graham

We Are Reckless
Christy Prahl

Always a Body
Molly Fuller

Bowed As If Laden With Snow
Megan Wildhood

Silent Letter
Gail Hanlon

New Wilderness
Jenifer DeBellis

Fulgurite
Catherine Kyle

The Body Is Burden and Delight
Sharon White

ALSO BY SHARON ROSE-KOUROUS:

Things Have Disappeared

How We Argue

In *How We Argue,* Sharon Rose-Kourous writes from the long
view of a life well lived and a world cracked open. Set against
the Covid-19 pandemic—and grounded in the northern
Midwest, in Ohio, Michigan, the weathering edge of Lake
Erie—this landscape serves her as London did for Dickens
or Old Florida for Dunbar: not just backdrop, but character,
crucible, and witness. These poems breathe in catastrophe
and exhale clarity. With wry humor and a quiet music, they
tend the compost heap of memory, sorrow, and absurdity. Her
metaphors surprise, her forms sing, and her voice never falters,
even as the world does. This is poetry that looks death straight
on and still notices the deer, the children, the way a flower
wilts or a flag endures. With wisdom that never preaches, and
a steadiness that never strains, *How We Argue* offers us what
we didn't know we were missing: a way to keep going, even as
everything changes, even as the last word is gone.

—RUS BOWMAN

Sharon's work is insightful, challenging, and creative. The
images in some of the poems that make up this volume will
resonate immediately with your own experience. These are the
reflections of a woman no longer in her "salad days," an old
soul with calloused feet and "an offering to the future." Sharon
Kourous' poetry magnifies familiar experiences, infuses them
with ambiguity, attaches them to universal realities, and
challenges assumptions you previously misinterpreted as
facts. I highly recommend *How We Argue.*

—NANCY SEUBERT

How We Argue

poems

Sharon Rose-Kourous

CORNERSTONE PRESS
UNIVERSITY OF WISCONSIN-STEVENS POINT

Cornerstone Press, Stevens Point, Wisconsin 54481
Copyright © 2025 Sharon Rose-Kourous
www.uwsp.edu/cornerstone

Printed in the United States of America.

Library of Congress Control Number: 2025940328
ISBN: 978-1-968148-00-3

Cornerstone Press titles are produced in courses and internships offered by the
Department of English at the University of Wisconsin–Stevens Point.

DIRECTOR & PUBLISHER EXECUTIVE EDITORS
Dr. Ross K. Tangedal   Jeff Snowbarger, Freesia McKee

EDITORIAL DIRECTOR   SENIOR EDITORS
Brett Hill   Paige Biever, Eva Nielsen, Reilly Crous

PRESS STAFF
Brianna Loving, Mydasia Zipperer, Ryleigh Miller, Sophie McPherson, Sam Bjork,
Madison Schultz, Autumn Vine, Allison Lange

These poems are dedicated to the care workers and scientists who helped us survive the COVID-19 pandemic; and to the many lives lost during that dire time. And to my children and grandchildren who helped me and each other endure those years with love, compassion, and laughter. Many, but not all of these poems were written then, as an offering to the future; as a way for the poet to survive.

And in loving memory of my mother, Betty Rose, who shared her love of language and learning with her five children.

How We Argue

Driftwood

There are slicings/splicings/scribbles
groves of scribes
de-scribing
a green life waiting, plaiting boughs of bud-
tips; winter is a napping where trees
compose themselves;
black lines scribble dreams in branches
undergrowth groans under,

waits what sudden spring
will unveil/unvine
translate tree-slate:

bloom blossoms; leafs' lines.

Then the slow cursive
time scrawls,
hides in heartwood below
bark, phloem, cambium,
cycle of years holds heart

wood tells time gone.
Time-trickery writes seasons
of wood-rings, whorls wind
wounded, cling
along lake shore wave/lap:
swash/wash flotsam
float some.

Some
cottonwood flails and falls.
One walker reads
its memoir.

Wave/wash waits,

my notes in the margins
written
in sleepy slopes
slip water-ward

swash/wash/phloem/
cambium.

A Lake is Good

Where you are when you get old
matters. You need to magpie some stuff,

gather glitter for picking over
on quiet evenings.

A lake is good because its shorelapping
makes silence easier. Collect some bling

bother with boxes,
shoeboxes of Christmas cards,

photos, beach glass, flotsam and jetsam,
matchbox covers from places you forget you knew;

fingerprints on windowpanes,
long slant of sun shining through dust

a cookbook or stack of poems
the open O of the absent moon

above ripple of wave against
obdurate limestone.

Aubade

There they are at the window
first fine fingerings of dawn

and all. Yeah, the birds
all one-footed on branches

singing their silly heads off.
And what the crickets

are on about, I sure don't know.
All fuzzy-mouth, me. Eyelid glue.

And any second now the alarm
will be alarming. Summer's long days

hold promise of heat, mosquitoes,
sunburn; only here in the few

short moments, not quite yet lucid,
it is time to wake from a slow sleep.

If the impending summer day
is mortgaged to the past,

please bring coffee and toast, lightly buttered,
and slip between these slightly rumpled sheets
with me.

River Raisin: Tecumseh Slept Here Too*

Ley lines, star-shapes, wave-lap,
and magnetic directions.

Think of the callousness of cities.
Skyscrapers: the word an example

in harsh consonants of what
we intend when we quarry.

Think: for every monument
of asphalt or stone, was also invented

a means of destruction. Gunpowder
or bomb. For every church, its cemetery.

Here we are cutting the grass,
or leading classroom lessons,

shaving or putting on ordinary feet
or in some bar with beer and friends:

average and simple, not asking much;
only some way to continue;

arms around shoulders we cherish.
Here we are in our towns,

not thinking exactly about lakes.
Or rivers. Or morning catastrophe.

Bird-shit on bronze shoulders:
George Armstrong Custer in moonlight.

*Tecumseh battled his way north to Canada, in 1813 passing through what became the small Michigan town the poet now calls home. A fourteen foot bronze statue of George Armstrong Custer dominates a main street bridge in this town, for reasons no longer proportionate to its size— or his place in its history. There he spent some of his childhood and met his wife. It commemorates his exploits during the Civil War, not his later enmity against Native Americans.

Atavism

If the morning mirror reflects you back,
count yourself fortunate. It probably means
those dreams that tumbled you—sleeping, slack-
jawed under the solitary touch of slow beams
of moon or streetlamp—were just atavistic gleams
of your invertebrate ancestors now creeping
under the blankets to rest. And you can come clean
with a smile or a handshake, reaping
the benefits of your fine education and keeping
the paycheck coming in: be grateful you're there
brushing your teeth before the daily leaping
thrust into sunlight, its wave-dappled glare
demanding your reluctant splash into reaches of air,
your gasping mouth pumping, your fisheyed stare.

Post-Menopause

Unfolding my children, shaking them out
to the blue sky, like white sheets,
I pinned them carefully to life,
& sat in the arbor
& watched them dry.

In the classroom where I worked,
it was the age of money,
& students looked like chessmen, lined
in stationary rows. In the afternoon,
they gleamed like gold.
Their anxious parents
bought the best lighting
available.

In my salad days I could have pitied
your bruised instep & callused feet,
& simple arches like curving skies,
& soothed them with my hair.
A foolish tradition.

Now there is only this old leather,
& ill-fit bones,
the bag which holds my folded heart:
an absence of warmth.

Lake Erie Dreams of Oceans

Wind out of the east;
far out the grey lake stirs
sends white waves
reaching where she walks
between wave-wash, beach glass, and bracken
black at the high-water line.

Sand firm, forgets
her feet the instant passing is complete.

Wind, long-reaching cold.
And there is no clear demarcation
between water and sky
at the far edge of vision.

Forgetting where she is
she follows the moonlight, the stars
the emptiness
in the air where an eagle was.

Is everything an edge?

Wave-roar in moonlight,
Lake Erie dreams of oceans.

Her footprints,
slightly toed-out and shallow in black sand

disappear.

Real Estate: FSBO

Between the studs and behind
the heat run:
dust, mouse bones, a cricket's
exoskeleton.

In August
a small green toad
waits
below the water spigot;

along the south side
bricks and ivy
sigh.

The house creaks more at night
and more in winter.

She had loved a man
whose thumb slowly
caressed
her quiet anxious palm.

Connections

How could we have missed
each other again? My refusal
to wear a watch
is relevant, but he swore
to wait all day. The directions
fell from my pocket,
streets acquired
a will of their own, changing names
in absolute disregard
of strangers or tourists.

This foreign sky
diffused the usual westward-pointing
sun, and my rental car
often followed the wrong lane.
I can see him packing;
gesticulating while furious hours
fall from the tower and
splatter like birdshit
about his ankles,
his perfectly shined shoes.

While I, now lost
on some narrow graveled
mountain pass, shift gears
and forget him
completely.

Duplicity

What is more astonishing than a rain-wet street
doubling the lights? Behind me like a snail's
path, it glimmers into silver. Ahead, the night
wears a water-sheen. And here I stand, still,

rain-soaked at zero. At the absolute no
where planetary spirals circle out and back
to the nimbus of the streetlamp's doubled halo,
I'm stopped, stilled at center; entranced by luck

or reverie to silence. I am timed
to timid stillness now. Black silver trail, a track
behind me and ahead: I remember lines
go past infinity before they double back.

With astonishing duplicity, all reflections show
those raindrops on his face— eternities ago.

Petrichor

Of the many sorts of rain,
misty is better
than pelting.

Seeds wait just below
a quarter inch of soil.
Moonlight

wanders darkly.
Dusky fingering:
precursor.

So many things can happen
between rainfall
and germination.

…

She clutches a
slender willow branch
beside the quiet waters.

So many kinds of rain
have fallen.
She knows them all.

Of Pocket-Lint

Because there is no place where god is,
she values pocket-lint,

and last year's fallen leaves
rotting in the stairwell.

Under the bureau by the bed
stray socks nestle
gently in the dust.

Like the old suit she wears
at every funeral,
she waits

somewhere in spare space
among spiderwebs and dead bugs
between the window-ledge and earth:

a flapping scarecrow
in no other wind.

COVID: the Early Days

This great human silence grows; we stay inside,
streets empty, stores shuttered, the great machinery

of commerce, of getting and spending, still.
Imagine a siege, a simple town, tall stern walls,

the castle keep guarded, the well gone dry, a flicker of flame,
the drawbridge closed. And this imaginary town

was once full of shouting, of children in corners playing, of
livestock and—

                  —-But now and then, a trebuchet

slams death across the ramparts. Those who die
are not necessarily the brave: chance and the moment

strike equally. So here, here all is silence. We move warily
six paces from one another, we realize suddenly how much

of what we thought we needed is superfluity, is fluff;
and that for which we hope, the human touch

is suddenly dangerous. Great silence makes a space
for skies to clear, for dolphin to sport in still canals

of Venice, for our air to breathe, for spring to find forsythia
and daffodils, for the timid deer in the woodland

to step out, long-legged and lovely, and browse among tulips;
this great silence gives back to earth its sovereignty:

our portcullis stays in place, while engines of destruction
wait. We quarrel at the well and hoard our food and
watch our neighbors die.

Shelter

Jumble of chairs sideways, blankets
pulled across. Pillows, toy trucks, a doll possibly
and books. A flashlight. Popcorn
or cookies swiped from the kitchen.
We, on hands and knees
crawling from room to room
in the blue/green/brown/purple light
the blankets made; we hidden
from adult eyes and ears,
—we sheltered in place.

Tree branches, a stalks from the cornfield,
bits and scraps of lumber, grass
dragged up and over the fence
and tied in place with rope
swiped from the garage; a rug
Gail's mom is looking for everywhere,
graham crackers, action figures,
a corner for the dog: my children
work all day building their spot
to shelter in place.

The tin shed in my back yard
damp and dark, spiders, worms,
the smell of rotting leaves.
A "Keep Out" sign; a list of "Rules"
a treasure map; pine-cone decor,
a milk crate rabbit trap just outside
and chalk-drawings on the walls.
Grandchildren with dripping popsicles
shelter in place.

We speak on screens, far apart
across oceans, from distant cities:
our faces boxed, our laughter unconstrained;
in the refuge of each other's distant love,
we shelter in place.

Ice

Ice trembling in a glass; its impersonal clinking
reminds her of nights in winter, the children all sleeping;
about her like a blanket, the silence, the lone
rooms, the cat or dog still, the settling mournful
"chuck" of the walls, insomnia stalking
hallways; and words, or their ghosts, working
in synapses where forgetting is usually stored
and memory sits silent, earning room and board.

Ice clinks in a glass, and the fingers about it
are chilled. Eyes understand but memory doubts
the actual and clings to the maybe; the ephemeral
phrase, the whisper, the touch more imagined than literal.
Hands clasping the glass warm the liquid inside
and the past is a place where truth slips and glides:
she believed there was love alive in the home,
then it changed: like ice melts, and is suddenly gone.

Ice chills in the glass and the condensate leaves
a rim or a puddle, and a ring that receives
a glare from the hostess. She tries a discreet
rub with her sleeve, then she quickly retreats
to the kitchen. There gather the talkers who talk and who wait
the appropriate moment to say, Ah, it's so very late!
and gather their coats and their hats and their gloves
and warm up their cars and their elegant loves
and head for their houses, with furnaces clinking
where children are warm in their beds and are sleeping.

She stands, with her hands still quite cold; still polite:
she nods to her hostess and heads into the night.

"Stay At Home" Order

I have become an old woman with wild hair
grey and unkempt, flying in the wind;
I have become that woman who brings squadrons
of brooms against dust-bunnies, but dandelions cheer

in my front yard; and my flowerbeds are groomed—
crocus open for my delight; and I am also she
who wanders out at midnight watching clouds
chase after stars, who entertains the moon

for midnight snacks. Let others chafe and groan
at solitude: I've cobwebs to admire, and deer who stroll
along the street as if it's theirs, I've unkempt hair
with flowers in it, and I am/am not—alone.

A Bundle of Accident and Incoherence Sits Down To Breakfast

Even when the poet is most himself, he is never the bundle of accident and incoherence that sits down to breakfast.
—Yeats

Halfway into my second cup of coffee
and with twice the recommended pain-pills
dissolving in my gut, I am able
for the first time in three days to bend
and reach the penny on the floor
which (the penny) all that time
had (from the center of a scarlet flower
of some sort in the carpet), mocked
my sprung back.

And then, there, realizing I've taken
the damn pills twice, I listen for my heart
to race, my lungs to wheeze and fold
inward like a vacuum cleaner bag;
and recognize my mortal self.
Will the autopsy reveal this lapse
of memory, failure to follow directions;
brain-fog senility;
will they nod among themselves
murmuring,
will my obit blame me—or science?

Who knows what deep part of the gut
generates knowledge of death or causes us
to whisper "I love you"
to any available listener?
To speak through the open window,
to shout, "I am here!"

The penny glints on my windowsill,
itself, solid and single
and only, only, only
its stubborn ironic copper-green self.

a.m.

If what you're peering into reflects you back
only mistily as a shower room mirror,
it's an even bet you're on the right track
toward your destiny. You'll eventually appear

as twin headlights of some night-passing car
brushing a window, or a nimbus requiring
a rage of insects, and ultimately a star
gazed at by former friends, themselves desiring

a less grave existence. So rub at the steam
and gaze into the place where you've noticed
less and less detail, where fade fractions of dreams
without distinction—it's that mist, be it noted

as you leave for work or return after an affair
that's patiently waiting, still keeping you here.

How We Argue

We

We come from slow flat places in Ohio,
places bumbling beside a river
or rising at a crossroads
after miles of corn.
The skies are big.
Our arguments are quiet.
Tight lips, silence,
an angry shoulder at the kitchen sink,
the stillness of wheat,
wind in a cornfield;
the stubborn small town
grassblade-in-the-teeth quiet
of Ada, Cary, Sandusky, Findlay;
the rivers: Ottawa, Maumee, Blanchard, Tiffin
shouldering through hot baked clay
to stubborn sullen Erie.

They

They carried nitro in their wagons,
nestled like eggs
in the rustling straw;
sitting hunched over reins,
patient, sullen, eyes-out for rocks
ruts, roadholes.
Trained to consider anger
a risky luxury,
they blasted roadways,
stumps of trees;
drained the swampland's silence
down to sullen Erie.
In front of post offices, on benches,
they quarreled silently
with their
recalcitrant land.

Home

My mother clenched clothespins
with her teeth,
hanging out the wash; moved
to the next task
thin-lipped and silent;
out of cracked grey clay,
insisted on
the reluctant beans, peas, berries:
she mouthing around the wooden pins
her arguments with God.

Ohio

The Maumee moves
through a stubborn land;
argues about limestone, treestumps, bridges;
in a quarrel with gravity
slips with muddy refusal
into sullen Erie.
The lights go on in small towns
along Ohio's rivers:
the gas station lights
the stop light
the tavern;
and out among the cornfields
the old two-window, wide-front-porch
brick farmhouses
fist their frustration
across the stubborn fields.

Shouting

When we shout
something really big is required:
God, a tornado,
the Depression. Our angers

tend to ruminate on porches
or lie wakeful
in the square of moonlight
on the blanket;
quiet anyway,
like the kicked dog
still running in his sleep
on the shadowed sill.

Shadow Puppets

Newspapers stuffed in cracks,
a blanket by the door, the house
coal-furnace heated, rattled
in winter winds; with snow
against the door, milk in the milkbox
frozen, pushing up the caps:
we quarreled for the cream.

Our mother made blanket-nests in chairs
and we sat with our books,
waiting to get well.
When the power went out
we made shadow-puppets on the wall.

Isolation keeps us huddled in our homes
(not much different now).
Sufficiency requires this:
mothers making nests for children
where safety circles them;
someone delivering groceries,
someone to wave
outside the windows;

some words
stuffed like newspapers in the cracks
of our fear.

Margins

The struggle is at the very edges of words
where black ink bleeds into the white, and margins
marshal like strict enemies. Rain beats on the windows
in a tempo of silence; the hours runnel into streams
with no significance. Trees are listening too.

Listening to the scraps of leaf and grass
the robin pastes together: a small wind tosses them
and the nest falls. This is the terminus.
Words will not wrap those frantic birds.

Nature wants to thrive—but the wind—
the language of wind speaks in branches
and offers no mercy; wind moves through
emptied streets of New York City; in Detroit
factories are closed and dust gathers
in Chicago; the language of silence blurs meanings
of words spoken laboriously pushed by fetid air
struggling in lungs where once words nested
at the very edges of life. White space. Silence.

Parked for the Duration

Here I am starting my 2014 grey Ford Focus in the garage,
the milage where it was 2 weeks ago
the Shakespeare bobblehead
still bobbing on the dash,
and I'm foolishly dusting the steering wheel
imagining driving almost anywhere but the end of my driveway
and back again.
When she was 12, my father let my daughter
drive his Plymouth Duster
down the long track from his house
to the mailbox and back—
she: thrilled, at the edge
of adulthood;
me: pissed he hadn't asked me first.

Here in the now moment at the edge of disaster,
—the limits of my range hardly
warm the engine.
I've shifted the weight on the tires, and it's cold outside.
The front-yard maple seems to lean
even closer to the grass where it will one day fall, its roots
a great entanglement of mud and tendril, its great torqued trunk
finally achieving rest; in the woods across the street a bluejay
insults the robins, and some yapping dog behind its fence
seems apoplectic.

No one's going anywhere. Dust will gather
on my grey Ford; the tree will lean farther;
birds have understood
no one will bother them, the range is theirs
and it's mating time.
In the great world where my bobbling bard will bring no laughter

where my granny-driving speed will not slow traffic;
in the hospitals of the world there is so much dying
in fear and solitude and silence; in the world beyond this quiet
tree-filled street, so much sorrow: I'm not going anywhere.
I collect a few pencils from the floor, a box of tissues,
a grocery list now useless, old;
shift gears again,
move again into the garage,
put her in park.

Correspondence During Plague Years

Dear _____,
Did I mention earlier anything about the world gone wild
nature rampant: deer on my lawn; birds mating raucously
eagles in treetops; and by the way, a buzzard went walking
down the alley this afternoon; have I said how the tree frogs
and toads are squelching about, looking for mates and food
not necessarily in that order? I think also I told you the dandelions
are bursting into yellow noise everywhere, and now I'm reminded,
the noises of cars and trains, motorcycles and loudmouth
males of the human sort are far diminished. Nature is having a go
at claiming back the everywhere: soon through the cracks
of I-75 North, there'll be plantain, bindweed, ground ivy
the common thistle, which I think is not so common
in its flowering; soon the traffic north will all be hawks
airborne avoiding the lake crossing, geese heading for home;
soon I -75 will allow burdock in the off-ramps, and the onramps
will simply crumble.

Canada's closed to us. Did I mention the groundhog? April
was never so busy; I hope the chipmunks underneath my porch
don't have babies, or at least not many. Where are the hawks
when I need them? And speaking of wild, I think my hair
will soon qualify me as a twin for the prophets of old:
I will speak of end times in a solemn voice and roll my eyes,
gaze heavenward. Alms? Alms for the poor? Should I try that
do you think? The distance between us, my dear,
grows wilder and stranger, and the times do not permit
long-distance visiting. Your face of electrons on the screen
is not the same. Your hands against the window are cold.

Yours, with love,

---

7 Dawns

There is no denying
the brilliance of sun
patterning her quilt
in stripes
and lines of shadows.

Branches move
between her window
and the sun.

Light slides
from pillow to the floor
muddled, discarded, forgotten.

Her slippers hold the imprint
of her toes in intimate
confusion,
stay shadowed.

The glass on the table
reflects a rainbow.
Every possible color
shivers in the air.

Should the world suddenly
shatter to its end
would she see its shadow
catlike
resting on her windowsill?

Would the willow tree outside
applaud
the clowning sun?

Newspapers

I'm taking a moment to speak in praise of newspapers
arriving on porches after a chain of events
so complicated and complex it's almost a miracle
that I can still in pajamas and slippers step out
and gather mine up without ever thinking of a person
rolling and bagging it and then moving around
under the stars or in the rain or driving through snow
to carefully toss it there; or the writers who thought
and reporters who reported, or the trees making paper
out of sunlight or the rain that watered the trees;

and thinking of rain I never consider the ocean
where it splashed on some far distant shore and then
became a cloud in that majestic and miraculous circle
I learned about in 7th grade; and then turned into
a chlorinated and clear gush from my faucet whenever I
think I am thirsty; and I don't need to think about
the meaning of rainbows splitting sunlight or the
spectrum of color that I can see but dogs
apparently see rather differently; and still in pajamas
and slippers sipping my coffee I never consider
the hands of the workers who bring coffee to my kitchen;
but sit still in pajamas, reading catastrophic events

that separate human from human and family from
family, and I consider the chain of possibility that miraculously
still connects us each to the other; the faces
of my far-away children, and the voices
ringing on balconies and porches singing for workers
who tie masks on their faces and enter the white light
of hospital rooms and make the news
that will tomorrow arrive unwished-for on porches.

Taffeta Prayers

Ice on sapling branch
window waiting rock

worm in flower's bud
beneath the woodwork: roach.

Newly frozen pond
finds the skater's heel;

devoid of color, the slight
kicked dog at doorway curls;

asleep in white-lit rooms
cure enters cells too late.

You, broken, drowned, despair;
your lungs forgot to live

machines pump putrid air
as cells commence to fail

eyes above the mask —
questions you fear to ask—

and all the lights will fall.
We decorated death

with anonymous hothouse flowers;
with sighs expending breath

spoke our taffeta prayers.
But always, always the stars

—were blazingly there.

Ventilator

Nose pinched shut,
lips clamped. Plastic tubes.
Inhale and hold.

Seconds counted.
Exhale. Again.
Inhale—hold
then expel all swiftly
completely—
More. Then more. Hold.

Imagine your lungs
as fragile pink balloons
perhaps drifting upward into trees.

One slight movement
in the unseen unseeable air,
and they will snag,
fail
fall limply slowly

past apple blossoms
past the knot
where a branch once broke

past the days when you
sat barelegged and proud
where a strong branch became
the saddle of your
sturdy steed, your apple-tree horse

and you swayed and rode and galloped ever
into the sunrising apple-scented sky
when you were immortal and young.

Grey

A crow pulls the black thread of himself into the roil
and movement—the sky heading toward us.
Flogging the town with time, a church
discards the hours: it is always 6 p.m.
Rain darkens the crosshatched streets
the small alleys, the path by the river.

River Raisin, slow and oily moves with stealth
wants to escape unnoticed. Under bridges and viaducts
furtive exchanges happen, and homeless with an eye
to the weather willingly trade
prayers for dinner and a warm place to sleep.

The beat of the bell sanctifies those reeking sleepers.
These streets so straight so square at the corners,
and the grey tolling of bells,
and the bleak of this grey:
we are a city of fools
who ask our churches to ring against darkness
who watch the skies seeking only this moment
who carry on our hands, in our lungs,
on our breath a dark sickness. We
tug the dark thread of self
behind us in alleys, along treeless streets.

Day 28 in Quarantine, Rapunzel

Of stones in the walls of her room, there are 672–each
cold to the touch, some are rough to her exploring fingers,
some wear fungus, some moss: the window ledge
though narrow, allows a view where the lake

stretches flat, and ripples like loss. The eye
of Erie watches her, she leans from the ledge
reaching for wind, her fingertips explore sunlight;
a shadow-gnomon covers 280 stones of her walls.

At sunset when day plunges suddenly into
stars: she cannot tell which are in the sky and which
float the waves; she marks morning on the compass
of her sealed unyielding door. She counts the stones,

the cracks between the stones, the birds that split
suddenly the air; she counts the cries of seagulls,
counts the waves that lap where her tower's base
marries the shore; she no longer counts the days,

having lost a word for days. Not knowing time,
forgetting language; her world this room, this light,
these shadows that rise and fall, the wind
that wraps the tower, the stones that wrap her room.

A sunlit wave becomes a word; mirage whispers a white horse;
a prince… or possibly stone 281 is a cure …or possibly all the stars
continue to fail as lake's moonpath leads
to horizon's edge— land and sky the same
indeterminate edge beyond

the windspread tangles
of her hair.

Empty Streets

The doorbell cameras are watching an empty street,
where heat-shimmers rise; a child's toy or maybe even two
lie scattered on the lawn like dandelions.

The mailman, masked, hurries up to leave some useless junk,
the trees grow leaves, lilacs are ready to bloom;
the doorbell cameras are watching an empty street.

Lamplight shimmers, a shadow or maybe even two
passes back and forth at the window; no one leaves
the house, and wafting through the air like dandelion's

seeds in breezes, voices echo along the empty street.
No one dares leave; in solitude, fears so quickly bloom:
what once was important now seems like useless junk.

What we want, we cannot have. This moment leaves
no glimmer of hope: we're watching an empty street.

The Masque of the Red Death 2020

"...through the six chambers: through the blue to the purple
through the green to the orange to the white and even thence
to the violet."
—Edgar Allen Poe

We never intended. Each of us had plans. It was only.
Enjoying the slow stroll along the beach, collecting shells
and sea-glass. Each day the sun measured time

as a casual exchange. Who knew? We wanted. Kept buying with
next-day delivery. We stopped using plastic bags.
It was working. Unemployment was down; the happiness quotient

like the chocolate ration, increased. We replaced our sedans
with SUV's. For safety. For prestige. Because we could and
the market was up for god's sake. America the exceptional

was great again. We went to movies, and married each other with
destination weddings exotic and important; we did. We could. And
the factories produced. And we wore clothes from China, made

by children whose faces we did not have to see, whose eyes would
never haunt us; we did not notice how along our southern edge
families died: they were not, after all, ours. We moved from room

to room: blue, purple, green, orange, violet, white, and finally, to black.
We never intended. Each of us had plans. It was only.
We wanted. The happiness quotient increased.

Slumber

Beneath my bed,
or in closet corners
spiders are silent
engineers of dust.

What they hear:
a whisper in my throat:
breath out
and breath in
slow susurration of sleep.

Dust listens:
soft sift
of detritus,
hair follicles,
sloughed cells:
skin converses with sheets.

Sheets rustle,
spiders weave silence,
undulating eyelids
seal my dreaming eyes.
Dustmotes
in moonlight
observe.

Nearby a maple
dreams a nightmare
of autumn;
a cricket speaks;
owl replies.

The house
groans and gathers,
floorboards sigh,
furnace breaths
warm air out
and cool air in.

Dawn

At my kitchen window
slow sun

as if
sliding
through Stonehenge

blocks out small monoliths
etches shadows
lays out minutes

divides seconds
into blades of grass
each shading
the universe.

Wiry gnomons,
define,
delineate

slice
a widdershins reverie.

Epic and forever
small sparrow-songs

rest in the dust
on the window ledges
of memories.

Zero

Slow accretion blurs our vision:
what once was clear drifts into memory.
Surface tension of water
floats only wind-tossed dreams; the rest
has settled in frozen mud.
The maple tree out front
seems to hold its muscles taut
fearing below-zero brittleness—
and zero dominates indoors,
books slipping from our fingers,
ideas dropping to the floor.
Birds quarrel at the feeder and deer
hesitate among underbrush.
We see what we wish to see, distorted
through the grime of wintered windowpanes.

The streets of every town are empty now.
With vinegar and some kind of prayer,
she washes windows, hoping for clarity.
Robins have returned;
the Carolina Wren flirts her tail; rabbits
uproariously chase through long bended grass;
squirrels gyre tree after tree. A V of geese
circles above the house, labors away.
Grass begins to green;
crocuses peer upward; tulips thrust their long
and hopeful leaves upward out of old debris.

Her face looks like a zero
peering through the glass.

Spring 2020: Fire

In February, the cold grass
leans and leans
crisp under
burden of old snow
blackened into grime heart-coating
and deep; winter
crawls along the fence
lurks below the porch,
curls like a lonesome dog
outside the many doors
silent and locked along
shuttered streets.

Memories of memories
smear in streaks down glass blurred
begrimed with residue of winter.
Daylight lengthens; sunrise begins
just before time wears out.
Flowers and birdsong nearly forgotten
replace the desolation of ice.
We awaken to lilac,
footprints in spring mud
by our many rivers,
rain wipes the grime
from city windows:

Up from beneath the long
winter ice of silence
a summer of fire follows.

Gardening at the End of the World

I clear leaf debris from tulips first
and daffodils, hyacinth, crocus,
and bring pliant drooping forsythia
inside so I can dine with golden petals
falling into my soup.

The crust of last year's leaves,
and wind-tossed twigs
I move with cold fingers
to the compost heap;
and gently touch the first small
yellow daffodil just tipping
from its slim green fuse.

In the house-warmed spot
beside the wall
parsley returns.

I have seed packets ready
even as I wonder why.

Virus

Dishwater scum gone cold:
silence sours the room.

Smudges record an absence
from the fake-leather easy chair.

Dust, carpet; slippers
hold coiled imprints of toes:

white feet, blue-veined, now lost
somewhere in some cold panting refrigerated truck

in some hospital parking lot. Lights always
on; yellow lines angle away from walls;

dandelions creep through aging sidewalks.
Shielded workers come and go

in plastic anonymity of masks;
the dead lie cold, stacked like sides of pork.

Sirens never stop. In every home an empty room
a tumbled bed, sheets sweat-sheened

blankets tossed, water dark and shining
in a nearly empty glass.

Beneath an idling truck, like snail-slime, a dark
wet tendril eases toward a drain.

Clearing Yard Debris in Early Spring

In fullest sun when the two rims of day
are equally apart, shadows' crisp edges
become mysterious lines: penumbra hedges me:
I rest my rake. On turned black earth, a worm
a moment earlier nearly sliced in two, reclines fatly:
curved, red-brown: a small alive thing safe inside its hour.

Over Lake Erie, air burns blue; horizon is lost
in the great curve of the world's arm; waves rest
while white air teases a mirage. The only deception
at this hour is light entering the iris of imagination.

Motionless, the worm accepts the dangerous truth
of continuing to live, while I, I gather imaginary lilacs,
daffodils, tulips. Though yet the earth I clear
is rimed with cold: what future hides within
the compact white stern buried bulb
whose center yearns to bloom?

Well Here We Are

Well here we are with the daffodils again nodding all over the place
and the crocus, and also forsythia waving their yellow wands
back and forth, not to mention the willows, and out in front
a duck couple waddles around looking like those cement ones
people everywhere used to put on their porches: it was a thing
I always wondered about; also the willows are bursting
and did I mention the rabbits? Well, let me tell you those rabbits
are chasing each other all around through the tall grass
and the thickets. And birds are everywhere: fat robins walking
with their little fast legs through the yard, and then, with their heads
cocked to one side spotting a worm; then there are the doves.
Well, the doves. With their mournful cooing and their really stupid
nesting where the wind will toss their mess of babies
splat on the ground; well anyhow all this springtime exuberance
is exactly what all last winter we waited for, this burgeoning
of growing, and the rain. Oh yeah, then there's rain which is always
raining on weekends. But this year, well this spring with its daffodils
and its lilac and forsythia and the animals all running about,
this spring is a season we simply have to—

Sonnet for Good Friday

Everything stopped. Preachers went silent between one word
and the next; buses groaning pneumatically stood practically still,
cars sat in driveways, cats on windowsills forgot the birds;
trees no longer burst into leaf, though the moon crept until

someone forgot to wind it; also motionless, the clock
waned into quarters; by the oceans there were no tides
rising in estuaries; and rivers closing their mouths, retreated back
into the mountains. No daffodils nodding and dancing beside

clouds, lonely or otherwise; no clouds. At weddings, no best man,
and funerals were too many and anonymous. It was clear
everything had stopped. The Pope alone in the Vatican
finally listened to god, who, failing to hear,
watched everything end, not responding to prayer.
We were afraid. Leaderless. Alone. Resurrection? Not here.

Dark House

"On the bald street breaks the blank day."
—Alfred, Lord Tennyson

The dark house that homes us all waits at street's end:
a candle shines at every glass, a flame that shows
some small voice, some thought, some message to a friend
passing in the emptied street, some fellowship that knows
we are not this, nor this the life we chose.

We are not this, we fear the way the world spins out
each islanded, marooned, and searching for some star,
each separate and lorn, and leaderless, and plagued by doubt
each country splintered, each port of entry barred:
in each dark house each candle flickers and goes dark.

The dark house that homes us all still waits, the streets
are silent and the night is still though April's naive grace
scents the air with lilac and birdsong greets
the Sunday morning walker, who with mask upon her face,
footsteps echoing, finds flowers in every space.

The dark houses along the street, behind their dark closed doors
sigh and stir; while earth returns to grass, and green, and flowers.

There is Nothing Unusual

Sunlight in rectangles
on the lawn
like windows into earth.
Shadows of birds
move across them silent, slow,

from branches
leaves hang limp,
and the tall sky
peers over a horizon
blocked for us
by a small gathering of trees.

From far, the buzz/hum
of a mower,
a hint of traffic,
the rude interruptions
a train makes crossing town.

There is nothing unusual.
The sun will take
the same boring path
from the back of each house
to the front;
from east to west across the sky
so similar today
to most other skies;

wrens fly back and forth
to feed their chicks;
shadows shorten at noon
and lengthen by evening.
It is all so predictable.

Except this plastic grass
heavy
over so many graves—

Nightfrost

Where petals go when flowers die
is sometimes a soft corruption,
sometimes annunciation.

She kneels, her knees
raw and scraped, her back an ache,
fingers so cold
she tucks them briefly inside her coat.

She kneels, gathering petals:
sun unbearable in the clear sky;
a bed of tulips, of daffodils,
of winking violets,
all gone, all brown, all wrung.

She gathers petals in her lap.
It's not just flowers.

Bodies are stacked in trucks, in rooms.
Graves undug, unremarked.

She knows,
holding the crush of flowers in her lap:
how cold the sun
moves northward, finding equinox.

Sorrow is a Deep Worm.

Blossoms unwrap
apples
grasp wiry stems.

Winds warp branches
skies darken, hail batters,
traffics death in orchards.

Along the asphalt road
rain torrents
eastward toward dawn.

Children splash
in gutters overwhelmed;
lawns are rivers.
Pumps wring basements dry.

Dracula-movie lightning
torments evening air.
Battered apples accumulate
beneath bent trees

where wasps will sip, grow drunk,
buzz raggedly away.

From one forgotten
gutted windfall,
slips
a silence,
burrows darkly into earth.

Here Beside the Compost Heap

Children's voices
like cries of sparrows
joyous
falling
wings spread.

Wasps
abandon dignity
drunk
on rotting pears.

The limp vine and wrenched root
of tomato spilling its
obscene yellow seeds:
like stars, they
constellate the slime.

Brown draggled feathers
yellow thrust of beak;
a slow heave of maggots
awaits the purity
of rot.
Articulate bones
measure limits of birdsong.

Maggots have finished.
Goldenrod bends and sways
above this perfect
scaffolding,
beak open
as if—

I grow comfortable with decay.
Detritus of memory rots
beside today's garbage.

There was a man who —
Damn! I've forgotten what it was.
Perhaps the way his toes
were cold against my feet
or probably not.

The slime cucumbers create
in old age nourishes
a tribe of ants. Were his eyes
blue? Did the night we—? Where was that?

The ants are lined and marching now.
I remember our feet hurt
as we trudged back to the
—was it a green tent or a blue one?

Tendrils of mold
flower
across yesterday's
apple cores.

The blue/black heave
of blowflies makes
a heavy blanket above
purity of naked bones.

Some young doomed
palewhite sprout
reaches up
toward sunlight as if

death
were a beginning.

I've only skin to separate
the fungi in my uterus
bacteria in my gut
from this steaming heap
where maggots thrive.

And Sometimes

And sometimes with my hand halfway
to the small green stem, I stop.
The cool break waits my fingers but I
simply can't. There are enough
flowers drooping in vases on tables
by windows, on kitchen windowsills
or surrounded by
half empty plates smeared with tomato sauce
cold pasta worming its way
toward the floor while children
silent
watch their mother at the kitchen sink
pretend
she's not crying.

And sometimes there is a catch
in a woman's
voice: some small violet
or dandelion even, some fading rose,
its petals gone white at the edges,
the center's yellow extravagance
dusting her fingers, and her eyes
focused far on the horizon —
or some edge of something else,
while a red bicycle
in sunlight heats and burns against
her memory.

And sometimes the slimy pulp of stems
too long in water rises green
and smells deep
like lakes, rivers, oceans;

or like a woman's voice
submerged but rising.

In Memoriam

for my mother

She once knew the most minute vein of each spent leaf
in intimate autumn. Then the leaves sang lullaby
until they were star-words. She wore disbelief
all winter while the sullen snow-freighted sky

weighed each disparate fragile branch, when dark
arrived at five o'clock and all the town's churches, their bells
brittle and cold, cast quarter hours out, and then went to work
on the long tolling days—the seconds themselves.

She once knew her way through the woods, and how a deer browsing
is a camouflaged thought, knew how her mind also kept
its thoughts to itself, hid in memory's inviolable housing;
she knew dreams remembered and knew while she slept:

elemental lace of a leaf wintered, weathered, still holds
the beauty it built in the sun, stripped and preserved by the cold.

Remembering Dun Aonghasa, Inis Mór
A triptych: ocean, wind, time

Though wind grabs her ears and strips wrinkles
from her face so twenty years slam against rock;
she can never be that girl again, the one
who nearly broke, the one who crawled
skin torn and eyes reft of tears; though the wind
hauls her young self back and makes her watch,
the bent grass and flagellant trees
are all new: and now straight-backed and old
she watches curve of sky, the far salt-wave, the stars
slip into dusk—and enters now the storm:
this womanself; her wind-blown hair.

This woman and her tempest hair: and always wind
always a breeze always the quick touch and sideways glance
across her sink where dishes stand where crusts of bread
fall to the floor— and that instant when wind
flattens grasses in a wave across a meadow;
there was always that impossible yield, fierce as flame
soft as light a million years falling
from stars dead before their glimmer touched on skin
—where this tall meadow holds the doubled shape
with drift of grasses in their windtouched hair.

Tempest-haired, gut-glued prone at the edge, head
thrust outward from the limestone, face wet with ocean,
spray flung against the cliff three hundred feet below:
in ancient days women barefoot and strong
scaled the cliffs in this ever-wind; eggs gathered in baskets
skirts drawn between their legs, naked toes gripping;

eyes grey as that invisible horizon where sky
and ocean write the edges of earth—

She rests against the sun-warm stone:

her mother, her daughter, her sister, herself—
as salt-spray rimes their hair.

Grassy Creek, Rossford Ohio

Beneath the bridge a scattering of teens in hiding
indulge the mystery of adolescent angst
and crouch with cigarettes and beer. They stay
late into the night, and then sneak home
through back doors or windows left ajar.
And then the creek murmurous and old,
drifts among the cans, lifts the butts, and carries Styrofoam
and who-knows-what along its way. Dead leaves,
and yard debris, broken glass, and hopes
half understood will litter the creek behind my house.

In spring the slow stolid creek will occasionally rise,
become a torrent spreading upward over lawns.
My house can sometimes seem a ship, and I,
I own horizons then, the onward rush is mine:
I'll out to Erie, ride the lake to Buffalo, slip
Niagara Falls, Lake Ontario, St. Lawrence—to the sea!
Off to the the Antipodes! Perhaps I'll spy the distant isle
where Ariel was found and lost by Prospero.

On the first warm day, garbage bag in tow
and ankle deep in muck, I clear a channel through
to let the water cleanly flow to Maumee's sullen
slow passage to the lake. I like a channel clear enough
to catch the glint of minnows as they dance. The teens,
washed out by floods will soon return: all water is
a moving mirror, a home, a dream, a promise
of a distant magic on some distant shore.

Portrait

In Memoriam, V. H.

Not flamboyant lines,
or practiced smile,
grey drift of hair;

but something about her lips
might once have been love.

Below her flesh,
the long slow build and arc:
sinews, integument, muscles
bone
delineate distances
between then and
everything else.
Even ... scars
or ... bruises
seen only by radar technology
or love
have disappeared.

Even the phone calls or silent evenings
even the well-intentioned cards and invitations
even the sloughed cells and fallen arches
even the glut of gut above the waistline
the book, the tv remote,
the dirty dishes the muddy shoes
the runneled cheeks or swallowed snot

all   scraped   away.

Hint of evening sky the curve

of walking by the river
a call of seabirds
one heron stilted in reeds
scent of mud rising in spring
or a willow slowly greening.

On the canvas:
only bones.

My Mother Descends the Cellar Stairs

Spiderwebs, messages in dust where bugs
scrawl diaries, cold and dark, damp;
newspaper yellowed on the shelves.
Jars of peaches dimly gold when light
shines through the open door: cherries,
pears—row on row. Wooden shelves
bend in the center with the weight.

She descends the cellar stairs pausing
at the last step. Glow of the coal furnace
flickers on the cement floor, and sometimes
sump water slides across. The dim light
seems heavy. She squares her shoulders,
the door creaks open, and she stands

deciding: peaches, pears, cherries
for dessert; peas or beans with dinner?

I sat with her so many days
beside the window, peach juice
running down our arms. Scalded skins
slid free, halves golden and sweet
slipped into jars. She'd stop
to watch a robin claim a worm
in the yard outside.

And so she stacked the shelves
with sunlight sticky on her hands.
Now she turns,
ascends the cellar stairs
with summer in her arms.

Still-life, with Apples

for my father

At the edges, first
ice clumps,
jagged,
loose
in lengthening light
drift and jostle
breaking toward the lake.

He remembers her name
but not why;
remembers the word
for grapes, forgets
sizes, colors, time,
the year;
remembers ice cream,
forgets addresses where they lived.

Blue eyes,
lightly rimmed
with red,
white legs, cloth shoes
shuffle

questing
along the hallway carpet,
cheerful floral walls.
He pauses to study
a still-life
filmed
with dust,

remembers one
clear day
tossing windfall apples
into the ice-rimed creek.

We Skipped Flat Stones

Sometimes across the flat rippled grey/pink/neverstill waters
of Lake Erie, sometimes when the sun is behind me

and stars circle still invisible above, the seagulls cry, dip, soar,
in voracious clouds: dive and quarrel all at once, and then move on;

sometimes I can see the far lights of Davis Besse Nuclear Power Plant
winking. I remember the beaches we swam, among silt and seaweed

the long slow shallows, the way, after a deep stretch where we on tiptoe,
were wave-washed to our ears. But after that bravado moment,

sandbars would guide us into knee-deep water fights, the dead fish floating
to the shore, where bloated and rotting they came to rest.

We screamed and kicked sand over them; as flies returned buzzing
and circling. Days were long, with summer's cumulus promise

of sandcastles and sunburn. Time lapped at our ankles;
we threw flat stones bouncing across the surfaces of waves

as seagulls circled and cried. Tommy and Judy and Grace and I
skipped school in spring, and headed to the beach, driving barefoot

past Davis Besse Nuclear Power Plant, past Howard Farms,
Ohio Rt. 2 guiding us, the yellow midlines flashing past, our laughter

at teachers and school and study halls tossed out the window
like discarded Milky Way candy wrappers. Time rested beside us

on the blankets in the sun, sand crusting our legs, sunset behind us,
the waters pink and purple and grey, heaving, dreaming in the dusk.

On this other shore, while eagles circle the heated waters from the power plant
I eye the flat horizon that intersects then and now:
distant wink of a light, the purpled waters, waves at my feet

marking the hour, marking the sand, tossing the bloated corpse
of a dead carp, scales shining and winking: a rainbow gleam;
time marking the distance a flat stone skips before it disappears.

Lake Erie Elegy

Torqued trees at Erie's edge
a great shattered cottonwood
sinew and gut splintered
ruined by wind.
Strong cells wait
water's inexorable
touch.

Ohio's Erie shores:
the slow slap
of wave on sand
shells, weeds,
detritus, dead carp,
cigarette butts, dirty diaper unfolding
like a rotten melon in the sun,
slipping in and out, rainbow
of suntan oil.

Childhood:
sunburned, snot-running, goose-pimpled
shivering, wearing lakescum,
sand grit inside swimsuit,
between toes; hair like seaweed,
fish stink.

The miracle of lunch
potato salad,
peanut butter bread smashed flat
cookies dropped and rescued
full of sand,
sweat bees, flies,
a heron one-legged, still,
a statue in the marsh.

Then tangled legs and wet suits
sandy towels, lake-smell
in our hair,
jumble in the backseat

as the great night sky
clamps over endless water;
we rocking forever, drifting
homeward, carlights lifting shadows
up and over above us
as we sleep.

Immense lake poised
where cottonwoods
and shattered limestone
sentinel her shores;
starlight balanced
on her waves, doubling
the moon and whispering
to the great migratory swan.

Enrico-Fermi Nuclear Power Plant

Eagle's glissando skims ice-crust.
Sudden sun-glints
diamond-bright.

Perhaps a swan, motionless;
while the deep waits.

Almost beautiful,
Silent twin concrete hulks.

Enrico Fermi sends white clouds
to climb the sky.

The great lake
gives no attention

to this momentary
disturbance;

nothing stops
its long contemplation
of the stars.

Walking Home

In the hot sun roadway tar slipped in puddles
to the graveled berm. She was a long way
from where she was, and the distance
hot and slow. She didn't know what
she didn't know and the smell of tar
muddled with dust of new-cut wheat.

It was a distant distance she went
and what she knew dripped as sweat-
drops fell and the sun was hot, birdsong
stopped. The Bono-Reno bus huffed
and roared on its way, and she
had a long way to walk
clutching a burden of books
against her chest, her shoulders hunched
bent against the weight, she under this
July or August sun. She was
a long way from where she was.

Cicada song in Ohio in summer rubbed
against her senses, she not knowing what,
huddled the books closer; the day
longer than a day, the whole sky hot
above her, corn-leaves rustle
and sweat-runnels in her eyes, she walked.
Unread books whispered: Nothing
is the way you think it is, and the sun
beat hot upon her, her footsteps slowly
raising dust beside the hot-tar road.

The Geometry of Cornfields

Cornfields: dark rough leaves
closing slapping overhead,
rows   rows   rows
in all directions,
green illusion,
geometry of solitude.

Distant sky and summer
all childhood long.
Trail of stars,
sky never entirely dark,
never alone.

Her August days swelter
below long dark green whisper:
harvest never her concern.

Tar melted
along edges of asphalt roads.
Children sometimes chew the tar,
stub their blackened toes.

They ran as blackbirds fly
through wheat:
bent stalks reveal their way
through endless gardens,
through and over,
around adult voices soft on summer porches.

Now she fails to see how at times

She failed

To see.

Rt. 20 from Toledo, West

Out Rt. 20 from Toledo, straight shot west: scrub oak, maple,
small stands of pine surrounded by flat, flat endlessly flat
fields of corn, leaves rustling a great green conversation.
Enclosed, surrounded by these whispering fields
old brick houses: two windows each side of closed door,
wide porch, two rocking chairs, slats broken, paint peeling, forgotten.

Silos sentinel the flat land; barns silently fail, petrified,
sunlight slanting through, thistles and nettles greening there.
Deep into the fields, far from the slow Rt. 20 traffic, occasional
beige stone mansions announce a shift from want to have.

Two-stoplight towns, a church on every corner; restored
train depot. Ohio holds on, rich and fat and flat, remembering
what never was. I want to drive that never-was road straight
west, I want rows of corn dizzying my eyes, I want
pig-wallows, horse barns, fields and fields of soy rising green.

I want schoolroom days,
hand over heart pledging allegiance to the flag,
bewigged wise fathers thumb-tacked above the blackboard,
to be the child who yearned to love her land
who rode smashed between older brothers
out Rt. 20, heading west into the sunset that never was.

We want what we never were; we are detritus beneath the bed
in fading houses where dreams dried out and hands failed to touch;
we are the scuttling centipede seen from the corner of the eye
as the hand just reaches for the towel; we are a motion
in the flour, the weevil in the cupboard cracks;
we are farmyard dust remembering rain.

Old Books

These books are old, dusty, brittle, untouched for years
moved from house to house in boxes I couldn't lift
they were so heavy, dragged up and down the stairs
bouncing and clattering, boxes I should have left

behind with other extraneous possessions, small stuff
collecting dust, mementoes of the places and the times
I no longer inhabit. There's more here than enough:
I carry everywhere old loves and sorrows, books with spines

broken and peeling. Paper: reams of it corners yellow, bent
paperclips—and lives as well: small red spiders live inside
covers of books, and tiny paper mites—and there are pages
where I spent
inordinate effort doodling, wrote lovers' names, or tried

in margins, argument with authors. I dust them and return
these shabby books, still well-loved, somewhat tattered, not
yet out-worn.

November

Whether it is earth tilting from the straight
line light always sinks to; or if that silent blaze
consuming itself moves away, in the low late
sun of November, I can't recall. A memory stays
of ping-pong balls in orbit in some dim grey
classroom; but time's complexities, unlike rays,
get lost in memory's curves. But it's always night
in space, I remember; light, needing a body, plays
through eons without illumination. As do we all.

What else is history but the occasional fall
of some body into light? In early evenings, low
haze decides shadows are irrelevant; dark sky forgets
to brighten cumulus; trees can't remember if leaves grow
independently, or if there's something they must do
to make buds happen. The slow river lets
its surface stop. In dark below ice, water crawls,
as light does through the void. As do we all.

Insomnia

Pacing the midnight floor
with gas or indigestion
or maybe heart attack
or because border patrol
puts children into cages,

beyond the safe rectangle
of her three a.m. window
shadows and stirrings
wear the mask of darkness—
and hospitals over-fill;

far trains call out
at every predawn crossing;
shadows of shadows
rise and fall in corners of the night;
everything she thought she knew
becomes miasma
rising from the lawn outside.

She opens the door,
enters the night

and all the stars are gone.

Small Towns

In small towns near Lake Erie
time ripples like shore-sand;
corrugates, accretes
as dunes do.
Shop-fronts revitalize
on small town streets;
river-fronts recover,
the newsy Chronicle dies
and no one notices.
World news enters sideways,
slithers in whispers,
sneaks under our pillows;
we ignore it all
until we can't.

Our lake, glacier-carved
and time-forgotten, lies polluted.
The slow slog of time let us ignore
corruption we didn't want to see;
the air we breathe
brings invisible pollution,
mirrors and reflects our land's corrupted leaders.

And we accepted, being busy,
the gradual diminishment,
malevolent accretion of evil.
And now we can't contain
the virus within—
though the lake, still in love with skies,
rises and falls, sends daily sunrise
golden over silent towns.

It Could Be Worse

Flat Ohio draws the language flat
to a lower level of risk: Nice day

we say to one another, nodding
six feet apart in supermarket lines

but do not say the sky is falling…
my wife has left, …my son is some war

somewhere I can't pronounce… the doctors think
the cancer is in remission not gone

but lurking…. It could be worse
we say in parting, passing on our way

to stoplights, small town centers
still hugging birdshit-laden statues:

bronze Confederate monuments, WWII soldiers struggling
to raise the flag, and names from Vietnam, Iraq;

where limestone Victorian churches
still rise from concave stone front steps

and steeple the flat sky. In Ohio we don't
struggle against language: our consonants

announce themselves without ornament;
vowels attain the graceless flight of crows

across dry cornfields; roadside ditches
lure repression toward a rainslick verge,

into a wheelspin rollover. Stark keen of sirens,
pickup trucks, engines running; perhaps a gun;

violence long repressed still silent; the sky sliced only
by the cry of southbound geese.

They Have to Take You In

You should see the black mold expanding
between the studs along the wallboard where
the paper's peeled back, and the shower leaked.

It's dark there, and there dust dreams of dead things
in corners and along shadows. If you touch
the damp area your fingers will send messages

creeping along wires and synapses until your brain
reminds your nose to wrinkle and you pull
your arm awa—or your brain does—without

thinking. You don't want to understand the crannies
under the concrete or the spaces between floorboards
where dander from your dog's hair feeds

those centipedes always just out of sight, you don't
wish to imagine the space behind the overflow
when you're soaking in your bubble bath each night.

You want only see the castle built of light
a spider weaves between the window and the screen.

Contagion

Everything converges:
length of day,
phases of the moon,
magnetic fields—
breath invisible in rooms
north sky aurora
politicians shaking hands.

In the tall blue sky
beyond the western edge
of Lake Erie: hawks.
Black and dangerous silhouettes:
they claim the silence all around,
follow star routes south.

In trees across the way,
a slow swelling of bud,
a slim possibility of leaf;
strong bones of trees await
transient blossoming.
Refrigerated trucks
converge in parking lots.

And everything converges
in the air beyond our windows:
aurora in the north
contagion in the east
hawks hunting as they move
below the faceless moon.
And in important places
politicians smile inside their masks
bumping elbows,
their breath
invisible in rooms.

Nitro: Its Uses

From the muck
of the Great Black Swamp
that bordered Erie,
forests grew: oak
cottonwood,
maple so dense sunlight
could fail to find a man.

Trees were girdled
farms followed,
cholera, fever
childbirth, towns, cities even.

The lake was a mirror
that forgot
Erie, Iroquois, Huron
oak, cottonwood, maple.

Nitroglycerin
straw-snuggled, in wagons,
road-ruts, swamp-muck;
men who held reins
lightly between fingers.
Roads blasted,
straight, true, level
steady
from Maumee to Fremont
to Port Clinton to Cleveland.

This aging body carries
my straw-snuggled heart.

Take one of these
the doctor said, under your tongue.
Call 911!

M-50 and Raisinville Rd.

To starlings clustered on the wire above M-50
the world is wind;

they enjoy the speed,
though motionless above the narrow world.

Sometimes
a worry strikes them all at once:

they rise into the air, grey with winter
and wonder if the end has come.

Below, cars wait for green
and then rush on.

Birds return speaking softly among themselves:
No. All is good.

The wind rises, touches each in turn.
They nod.

The narrow ribbon is the world they know;
the wind their home—the grind of gears, the trucks

the tops of cars below: the families who move
from unknown past toward some future dream

prove to the birds: now is now. The road's
a moment in the dream.

Aligned again, they sleep.

The Aforementioned Centipede

When you're naked and about to step into the shower
and a centipede runs out from beneath the mat
you can't help it, you scream and dash out of the room.
This morning I killed one by showering it full strength
with hot water and I still don't want to get naked again
but I can't exactly buy a different house with
a blue bathroom instead of my green one and anyhow
if I did there would be bugs in the floorboards and
mice in the walls because most of us have no idea
what gross lives take place beneath our expensive carpets
and our newly redecorated entertainment rooms or
home theaters or whatever upscale need HGTV
has taught us this season. Here in lower MI with
zip codes 48161 and so on, we built our towns splat
on top of the Great Black Swamp which once drained
into Lake Erie and supported a great variety of wildlife
which today is mostly visible in our mosquito population but
which also creeps up our drainpipes and into our showers
like the aforementioned centipede for whom I
in my nakedness was probably a terrifying large pink
blob reaching for the hot water. And so although
the survival odds were in my favor and although I
was immoderately frightened by his many-legged swift
run about the soap ring in my tub, I owe at least
the apology of the colonialist who, having callously wiped out
the indigenous population, now centuries later
out of supplies of smallpox-laden blankets anyhow
and trying to cope with the poetic justice of COVID,
only now tries on the white-guilt business of being sensitive.

Lansing, MI: 6 ft.

Between us the distance
is more than 6 ft. Me not breathing
your air, you not breathing mine
is hardly sufficient.

Every place my six feet of space encompasses
is where I inhale such a sorrow as fills
my lungs with loss.

I don't know how to count the empty
hollowness of families,
who left a love below 6 ft. of earth.

Across the nation around the world the empty
circles, 6 ft. apart, lifetimes lorn,
we distance from each other, inhaling grief.

Each in our separate hollows, me not breathing
your air, you not breathing mine
you infected with hate

and waving flags and carrying your gun:
the distance between us
never sufficient.

Delivery

If Michelangelo's David
should ring my doorbell,
perhaps wearing UPS polyester brown,
and heavy oxfords,
I'd jump him in the foyer.

Boy with a man's eyes;
confident, reaching,
judging distance;
knowing without thought
how the stone will strike just so
right where the brow furrows;
knowing as a body knows
how a foot must angle
an ankle turn, a finger–touch–
and then move on.

I'd offer him the crumbs
of last night's brownies
stale on a flowered plate
beside my bed; surely
such a man-boy
still loves brownies?
My sheets are scented lavender,
with hint of chocolate brownie crumbs.

Of course the Renaissance had to happen
with boys like that
strolling through the town. His feet
are pale and arched and strong
legs muscled, steady, sure.

Michelangelo must have
loved him, caressed him from the stone.

Lansing, Michigan April 15, 2020

I want words that will will break something
words with power to smash to hurt
words with force —
— pacing the room swearing at the tv screen.

Those with power to save us
seek self aggrandizement;
and the women of science, the men of medicine
bow and curry favor

while nursesanddoctors die
husbandswiveschildrengrandmasandgrandpas die
brothersandsistersauntsunclescousinsfriendsstrangers
thoseinhomesandthosewithnohometogoto...

(In Washington, they play the game
of power moves; avoiding blame
while people die. It's all the same.)

I wait at midnight in the dark for words that rise in night
for the words of my fear of my loss for the words to say
once as a child I loved this land and once as a woman
I believed the story of the story of who we were;
the story of a people
generous and tough and often foolish and often unkind
still trying still growing still becoming.

(in Washington they play the game
the Capitol— they tried it here; it is the same)

The impotent man coughs a dry cough
and turns in his bed to face the wall:

(between the motion and the act
falls the shadow)

all the king's horses and all the king's men
will fail our nation's need again

I want words hard enough to say this:

We turned away:
when the sick said, *Help me,*
we did not answer.

Here in the Midwest in this flat basin carved
by a timelost lake and enriched by a great black swamp

an industrious and strong and sometimes stupid people
burned trees, hacked undergrowth, plowed land, planted farms

went to war, came home from war, moved to these cities,
raised raucous children—all growing richer and stronger and fatter

and planting more land and buying more cars and
vacation homes up north and pickup trucks that often
flew the confederate flag

for no other reason than to proclaim themselves tougher
meaner louder and not ever impotent, not ever fearful
of the banker or the banker's wife

not ever answering the professor the scientist the doctor the teacher
but always gunning the motor louder:

these ordinary people: privileged strong loud
ambitious, sometimes kind and often foolish,

they got in their pickup trucks and drove to Lansing
to show the world their trucks are loud, their manhood strong,
no woman can tell them what to do.

and all the king's horses
                    and all the king's men
                                        carried home their deaths…

FINIS (as they say)

FAQ

When the empires of the earth speak of immunity,
indigenous peoples answer
> smallpox
> measles
> venereal disease
> alcohol
> opium

When the great white nations speak of inoculation
people answer
> slavery
> manifest destiny
> trail of tears
> wounded knee
> penal colonies
> Tuskegee
> Guangzhou
> Calcutta
> Peru

When the scientists tell us "contact tracing"
we answer:
> history

When the capitalists tell us "progress"
earth answers
> Himalayas
> whales
> cod fish
> white rhinos
> plastic waste
> the oceans

When earth says: here is a new virus
     we say
               let's swarm the capitols
               let's go the the beach
               let's open the factories
               let's have a 4th of July parade!

Virus answers: Done.

4 July 2020

We think all those troops are replaced by their names
engraved on a wall, a parade, a video clip,
a tee shirt, a cheap plastic flag, or the claim
fireworks make at night. Later we slip

quietly between bought sheets, uncertain of dates,
dying into political quarrels. July ozone
oozes in windows while the occasional late
cherry bomb explodes— we sleep past the well-known

adage about history. The best Covid holidays
happen on weekends: fools on highways and beaches keep
excess population controlled. Pyrotechnics replay
on every channel, while even houseflies sleep

unaware they once were maggots. One-day patriots share
this ignorance—and yet— …the flag is still there.

Penelope to Odysseus

That was no business trip; gone so many years
I forgot your face; I forgot the way your back felt
beneath my fingers, how the scratches I made
marked you mine; I forget the roughness of whiskers,
and the heavy step on the lintel; I forget your wet clothes
lying where you tossed them; I forget your snot
spraying out whenever you coughed I forget
the way you snored through the long nights
of colic when Telemachus spat up until my shoulder
reeked; I forget the way you rolled over in our bed
without asking, without foreplay, without affection
with only need —yours— and the way you slept late, sated,
and your breath reeking of wine gone stale.

Now you show up homeless, lying about your identity
and making yourself at home; showing the door
to all my friends. The waves which lap these shores
are not the waves that carried you away; the waves
that slapped the shore and slapped the shore and slapped
the shore while time unraveled, wove, unraveled, wove
while the sea changed, changed utterly. The olive trees
are old and bent, harvest gathered year by year
and pressed, and gathered yet again. Your dog, Argos,
gone grey, sleeps in a corner, pisses in his sleep; rheum
gathers in his eyes; he tail-thumps at every stranger
so your pretense means nothing. It could be you
dragging your ass home at last, arrows limp in your quiver;
 it could be someone who buried you on some small island,
or one who knows you're cavorting with some aging temptress;
or one who remembers you as the pig you always were.
It could be you (one of many) who knows
the secrets of my bed.

You think I've been weaving your shroud again and again.
You never did see me. You never saw *me*,
so think whatever pleases you. I've hiked the hills of Ithaca,
sailed solo around islands near and far, sunned naked
on beaches, shared wine – and more – with some;
frightened other suitors from my doorstep,
and having made it mine –this solitary life
suits me perfectly.

So. Make yourself at home.
You'll find the place a bit run down.

I'm sailing on the tide.

Field Survey 2050

Ice-rime. Shores. Seagrass. Gulls.
Grey rocks are coral so old
they remember the fingerprints
of god before he was born.

Sunlight only a moment brighter
than distant stars.
Overhead a brief gleam
might be a comet
might be debris.

There was a time
we imagined flight
beyond the limits gravity
clamps about our ankles.

Jail cells imprisoned mostly
white collar criminals or
former mayors of cities
like Detroit in the before time
when cities were a thing.

Each now islanded.
Each small stone.
Beaches smell of fish-rot.

Behind closed gates
doorbell camera
Guns ready.

We watch the littered shore

and the crying empty wind.

Vignettes

In the world's parking lots refrigerated trucks
like cattle feeding shake and cough
night echoes this sound.

In a supply closet an exhausted nurse
sleeps upright on a wooden chair
drool dampens his mask.

Ambulance traffic jam outside hospitals
families watch the lit windows
one imagines a vulture, dead branch, soundtrack.

In the night, no airplanes
wake the sleeper where oblivion licks her neck
but crickets and tree-frogs shatter darkness.

In our dark houses,
our opulent hopes no longer matter.
The things we bought.

Our leaders lie awake thinking,
fuck, I never asked for this,
and pummel helpless pillows before they sleep.

Snow out of season
surprises April
and blankets all the new-made graves.

We Had Walls

In winter it was buy bake make sell do work it was commute;
in February ice-ball hours snow-packed we were cold we gloved
and booted worked with walls scraped and swept
high-piled and cold black below, buried, and dark.

Silent we were in bleak; the slowly north sun
gave days hours, but we kept cold. We were moon-haloed
in March: it was before, but dawn gleamed blue and sky
remembered green; riverside willows drew long yellow lines
wavering above footprint trails soggy with wet. It was not
yet spring-possible but the probable sprouted pale rising
below leafmold. It was buy bake make sell do work it was
commute, it was office it was save scrape pay borrow.

It was whisper warning contagion of doubt; it was politicians
was palaver was not-news fake news other words other ways
it was far it was not here; where plague whispered in foreign
language, not ours not us it was not us it was there; we
were safe it was still buy bake make sell do work it was still
exceptional us. Death in a language not ours
called. Not us we were Americans, we were ourselves our own
bastion of good; we had walls we were commerce and profit.

We walked into spring done with dark
we opened our doors wanting birdsong and flowers:

we waited the wait we wintered we bought and we sold
it was buy bake make sell do work; it was party was play
was to hell with the truth. — Then we looked into mirrors.

Reflection

If the mirror you gaze into morning and night seems misty
perhaps that's the message. You're fading toward that future
you'd love to avoid: the words you write with your finger
say good morning it's probably just a
slight case of indigestion. Or are you gradually fading
out of focus with the world, having a tough time relating

to the six a.m. news and its incessant moments of history
pounding your brain, your coffee still, still; your synapses sleeping
and the things you knew, you know now seem a bit out of focus.
You peer at the mirror and wipe off the glister
trying to find yourself, to secure some sort of locus
for your indeterminate anger, the reason your gut's always keeping

you wide awake on your empty kingsized bed where there's room
for another and the empty space is depressing
because there's no dent in the sheet, and the world seems doomed
anyhow by government failing and flailing and keeping you guessing
about what you once knew for certain: this land, this place you call home
is destroying itself. The steam slowly rises. And then it is gone.

Moondark

I'd sidle slyly out if I were wiser,
and, shadowless on the moon's dark side,
contemplate my absence in the wider
perspective I'd learn from such silence
as stars keep. Like that cold rock, blind-sided,
I should look always away as the dimlit view
recedes in time. Silence waits where shaded
mute rock knows me as I once knew
the cellular song of the maple's crimson leaf
as autumn encroached; and the leaves sang
until they were grounded. They whispered disbelief
all winter like Orpheus, wind-drifted and wan
with lunatic voice, words remembering song—
but scattered and senseless: dark side of the moon.

Lake. Ice. January.

Those who say winter is bleak
have not considered closely
or followed
crosshatching bird prints
—different on ice
than in refractions of flakes—
or the not-sun pale
glowing upper air.

Of greys
there are multitudes
deep in undergrowth
dark

then suddenly
fracturing
lifting;

there are also greys
clouds leave
in their passing and roil;

there is white disguised as grey
rising from ice
where the lake
holds fish in stillness
and solitude
until

—eagle!

a black instant
within the grey
of her hunger—

fish

gleams dripping and bleeding

in her talons.

Black Swamp Meditations

This Ohio flatness gives voices and visions
that slow patina of black swamp mud you might
still notice as footprints on an expensive new carpet,
or at night under chemically green lawns, as decisions
to reinvent the clover. In river's revisions
of its own path, this flatness is time's quite
natural advantage. In Ohio, one's sight
is stumped only by clouds and roof-broken horizons,

so the old mud below must serve for memory's
stubborn refusal. Miasma, its midges
and malaria-breeders, lies waiting where obligatory
ostentation lines river-town paths; and its ditches
still leech down to the shore, send Erie
the same old swamp-stuff its sewage enriches.

Epiphany

Where water meets shore, each wave is an epiphany.
The eagle who seems so still where branch meets sky
understands a concurrence of need and opportunity.
At the shoreline in a tangle of dead weed, shells,
and sea-glass washed smoother than prayer,
a swiftly disappearing toad leaves a dimple in the sand.
Everyone knows our understanding of the moon
is sometimes round and sometimes only a sliver of light
and sometimes a halo circles it. Stars are moments in the sky.
Everyone always understands the human, self-aware and foolish
walks like an alien among the green grasses.

We all wanted
we all wanted more
we wanted what they had
we wanted everything they had
we wanted to possess everything and we did
we possessed every thing.

—The fool said to the rich man:
"What you have is nothing. Nothing comes of nothing."
And went walking into an aurora of northnightsky.
—She sits in the salon drying her fingernails
and thinks about dinner.
—A man in a shabby blue woolen coat
is collecting bottles and cans from the garbage.
—One is mowing the lawn and imagining his hunting camp Up North
and a dog barks endlessly trapped behind a wooden fence.
—A child runs arms outspread in the wind
along the rainbow path toward sunset.

This is the way the world will end.

Everyone knows an epiphany gathers no moss,
and the dreamers and poets the prophets and schoolteachers
should be gathering bank accounts and mortgages;
manicures and lawns—
everyone wants everything, and every thing
gathers like lakewater where land and water
have an understanding, an acceptance, an epiphany.

Mise en Abyme

There's such a stillness in the town you could hear
a pin drop if anyone were dropping any pins anywhere;
there's such a silence and the stores are shut:
the windows' blank stares invite a stone to crash
if anyone were tossing stones anywhere;
there's such an absence one could count
from zero backwards if anyone were counting anywhere.

In grey skies weighted with the absence of snow
no jets fly, no contrails, no lights at night. Nothing winks
in the grey waters of the grey lakes, no fishermen casting
a thread of hope into the zero that water makes when struck.
In silent houses children are doing their best to be children
while their parents engage in futile tasks as all adults
must do; and the dogs are waiting for walks and in bowls
goldfish circle aimlessly looking for meaning among plastic fronds.

There's such noise in Washington D.C. where less than zero
happens, and the proud and the foolish gather pompously,
each the mirror of the other, like those mirrors on opposite walls
reflecting endlessly, echoing echoing echoing...

Voting 2020

I'm not your Lady of the Sparrows
you loud and quarreling
ugly noisy rats-with-wings
—not your St. Francis speaking in
birdwords; not your beneficent
scatterer of fieldcorn.
Squirrels stay away from my door.

I'm not your soccermom making time
for pedicures, not your cookie-baking
blacklives hating lean-in woman.
I'm not the kind lady lives here
hoboes made into a myth.

This is my place where weeds meet Roundup
where old women
gather and snap beans like they were skinny penises.
This is my stakehold my guiltless
apple grove. I am not Eve.

How do you like my hysteria now?

Watch how you fucking talk Mr. Senator.
Your twitter's putrid scold is done.

sometimes alone with summer's end skies blue and
astonishing is ok; the small white clouds seem innocuous
and light. rain greens the brown grass and the clover
waits for rabbits; the voices in the distance are gentle
and friendly and not talking to me alone here at the end
of the street during the end days of my country.

I carefully completely unfold
my vote-from-home ballot
circle black ink
inside the lines,

delete the zero in the Oval.

Jan. 6

Faint resistance between my teeth
then summer:
tongue-drenching
cool, sunshine and earth
trees and meadows

purple/red
dusted faintly
with evening bloom.
Juice runs down my chin.

On the tv screen
a man in uniform,
tear-runneled voice:
"I expected to die that day."

I eat grapes
and worry about
fitting into my jeans,

transfixed

while four men speak
of eyes nearly gouged out,
(like grapes!)
of concussions and smoke
and fear, death,
and confederate flags
American flags, pain

as they stood,
and saved America.

Again.

Resist!

In this hall of mirrors
there's no easy
way to look;
it's a madhouse and you
blindly walked in.

Close your eyes for a moment
and you'll be with Alice
and the mad King
in the insane mirror
in our distorted world.

Choose instead
the slant tipping
uneasy angle of repose
in the anti-gravity room.

Resist the dizzying force
of what you see;
trust gravity.
Stand upright there,
Askew to appearances
but holding your own.

Afterward

Paint all your mirrors black. Close
the blinds, take all the lightbulbs out.
Wait for the new moon. Your blank clock shows
it's time to leave. Discard your doubts

in the shadowed hall. The tree-limned sky
closes, the last star fails. Listen to your feet
on the gravel. Only you move in the wide
empty earth. Only your face illuminates

the darkened street. Yet in the moon's silence,
you see everything. Behind you, the door
closes, the windows sleep, walls unclasp
empty mirrors. Nothing more

than shattered glass alerts the moon's dark pull:
you hear insistent seas, distant, slow.

Morning Glory: There

's
no stopping
a pale tendril in the rock

's
weakest moment
the wall

's
vulnerable stucco where rainseep
's
quiet invasion

began; or along the rusted fence

into the tree
's
low innocence.

SUDDENLY

blue bloom
's
everywhere he

touch
ed

her skin
's
memory.

Pocket-lint persists

in jackets smelling of mothballs on Goodwill racks
sorted by color and sizes, shapes
of men now dust in graveyards.
Pocket lint lines tight jeans
and hip-slung, slouches along
lorn streets.

Towers in New York disappeared
in sudden clouds
condos in Miami
crumbled in the night
families burned in London
refugees in Kabul/ Gaza
U.S. southern edge
lifted toward empty sky.

In Turkey and Syria the air
filled with snuffout dust.

Dust everywhere
settled in gutters grew grime in alleys
transmuted into tulips

drifted across seas in oily slicks.

We walk
fingertips lightly
dusted.

Pocket-lint.

Lost

The house is dark. Its floors collect
all those autumns. Leaves in the stairwell,
buckeyes, shells of seeds, the dry scat
of foxes, coons. Chipmunks rattle
inside its hollow walls. Lights of passing cars
cast blue ghosts across littered shelves.
His voice lies broken by the door.

Hollow of bone and swift of sight,
exhausted by stars' faint trail
I gather twigs, come in our window
with bits of grass, the glitter
of a dropped ribbon, the silver trail
of a slug. Through shadeless glass
the moon leers. And I am home.

Here among rotten leaves
and faint echoes of piss,
I recognize myself. How I was.
How I was silent, how silence
became the way we spoke, how anger
lay like dust in corners, how futility
gathered beneath the bed, and how I lost
the syllables of words.

Resting in his ruined easy chair
I forgive nothing.
Combustion smolders among shallow leaves,
sours the ceiling, chars floorboards,
slumbers in that ruined easy-chair,
spreads sharp-tongued conversation
along the silent halls:

This is the language of joy
glowing among the litter;
this is the voice of the lost
returned,
a flame among the syllables.
This is the language
I carry out my last window
into the shivering dawn.

Eastward

I will grow old eastward,
wind-wrung in one direction
while the world's winds part,

rise up over rocks,
carve my rough bark with rain,
rest green moss there;

and my bones will grow slender,
sunlight will shadow through them,
gnarled, bent inward, curled,

growing more slenderly
passionately lighter all
shining

in the same
direction.

There was a river where I played
while my grandmother,
sitting on a rock,

her thighs solid, knees spread,
fingers delicate enough,
threaded a worm

along the shining hook;
and in one swift intensity
arced line, bait, sky, rock

all in one direction;
leaned into the wind
as though she were

a tree.

Beach Glass

Outside it is snowing again
and the footprints of my yesterday's leaving are obliterated
in the today down/whiteness of no sun,
no since, no ever, no then or was,
in the air-filled understated blackness of trees.

I have always left a trail
slightly toed-out and sort of scuffing,
or backtracked—
circling about some stray meadow
or alongside failing Erie's shores
choked with rip-rap, with cement;

green waters sloughing
from slick mossed trilobites,
themselves amazed to be still here
in this new light;

and licked by pollution,
lost in limestone, stubbornly retaining self.

I gather these fossils,
time-retaining shapes—
fruition of years like a snail-slick,
like beach glass shining,
fragile, suncaught,

gone.

Walkabout

Morning snow lay on each branch,
where old trees rustle
in a cold wind.
But sun's warm hand
did a lover's work,
then disappeared
as lovers often do.

If you should see an old woman
walking north
and north on side roads
through Michigan,
heading for the great green
forests of Canada,
shoving her walker
up hills, riding it down
arms wheeling
off-key song trailing—
hand her a coffee and a chocolate bar
as you speed by.

Later look for her in some sunlit clearing
tucked under fallen leaves
her roots and tendrils
reaching into the earth.

ACKNOWLEDGMENTS

Gratefully acknowledged are the following publications, where earlier versions of poems appeared:

Melic: "4 July 2024," "How We Argue," "Lost"

New Ohio Poets: "How We Argue"

Octavo: "a m"

Comstock Literary Review: "Eastward, Lost"

The Formalist: "Duplicity"

Piedmont Literary Review: "November," "Still-life with Apples"

Savoy: "Atavism"

Terrain: "Eastward"

With loving gratitude to my parents and four brothers, for a childhood made rich with love, laughter, and books—always books. Their tones, cadences, and idioms of the Midwest are still mine, as are the stubbornness and quiet stoicism exemplified by neighbors who helped raise us. The title poem of this collection reflects the understated values, repressed emotions, and stubborn persistence underscoring my family's history in Ohio's rural communities near the shores of Lake Erie.

My daughter Helen and her husband, Denny, and their daughter, Lizzie; my son George and his wife, Oona, and their two children, Sofia, and Nikos, have all enriched my life beyond measure. In my adopted Michigan town, a circle of wise activist women supported me when I ventured into prose, and welcomed me into a sisterhood of shared values.

And I owe sincere gratitude to Nancy Seubert and Rus Bowman who each took the time to read and review an early draft of this collection. My thanks to senior editor Ellie Atkinson and her group of meticulous young editors who combed through these poems, finding errant commas and freeing lines from double-spaces between sentences; and to the cover designer, Allison Lange, my thanks for an image which fits perfectly. And to Dr. Ross Tangedal, Director and Publisher, who brought it all together.

Sharon Rose-Kourous is a poet and former teacher who taught high school literature and language arts, spending most of her career at a suburban public school. She is the author of *Things Have Disappeared* (2024), and her work has been published in *Able Muse, Melic, The Formalist, Comstock Review, Piedmont Literary Review, The Lyric*, and many other publications. She lives in Michigan.